GLASS

BookLife

written by
Harriet Brundle

©2016
Book Life
King's Lynn
Norfolk PE30 4LS

ISBN: 978-1-910512-82-1

Written by:
Harriet Brundle
Edited by:
Gemma McMullen
Designed by:
Drue Rintoul

A catalogue record for this book
is available from the British Library.

Contents

The orange words in this book can be found in the glossary on page 23.

What is a Material?

Materials are what things are made of.
Some materials are natural and some are man-made.

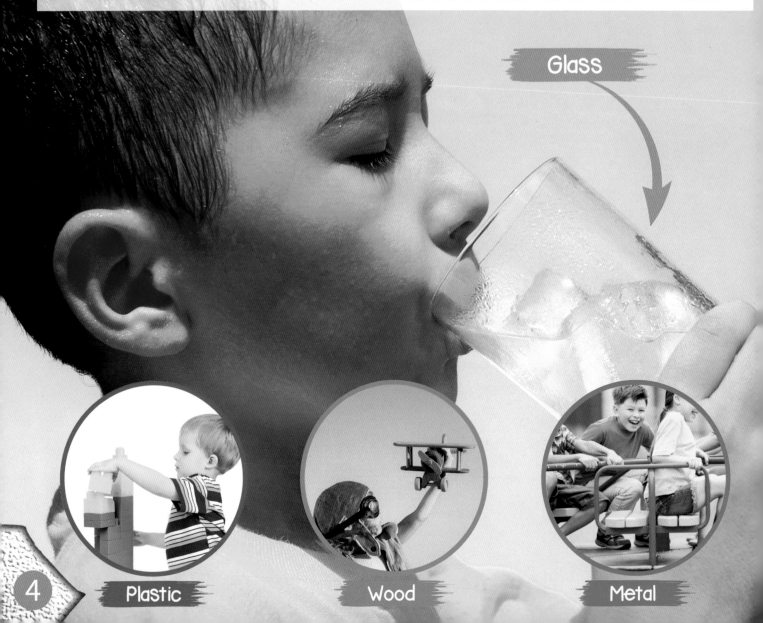

Glass

Plastic

Wood

Metal

Every material has its own properties. A material might be very soft. This would be one of its properties.

Pyjamas, cuddly toys and pillows are all soft.

5

What is Glass?

Glass is a solid material made from sand. It is man-made.

TRY THIS!
....
Have a look around the classroom. What can you see that is made from glass?

Glass is transparent, which means we can see through it.

Properties of Glass

Glass feels smooth to touch and it does not bend. It can be strong and not easily broken.

Strong glass

Glass can also be weak and very fragile.
If a vase is dropped, it will shatter.

Vase

BE CAREFUL!
Don't touch
broken glass,
it can be very
sharp!

9

Uses of Glass

Glass has hundreds of different uses. Strong glass is used to make windows.

These are called panes of glass.

Glass is used to make bottles and jars. They are very useful for storing food and drink.

Glass in Water

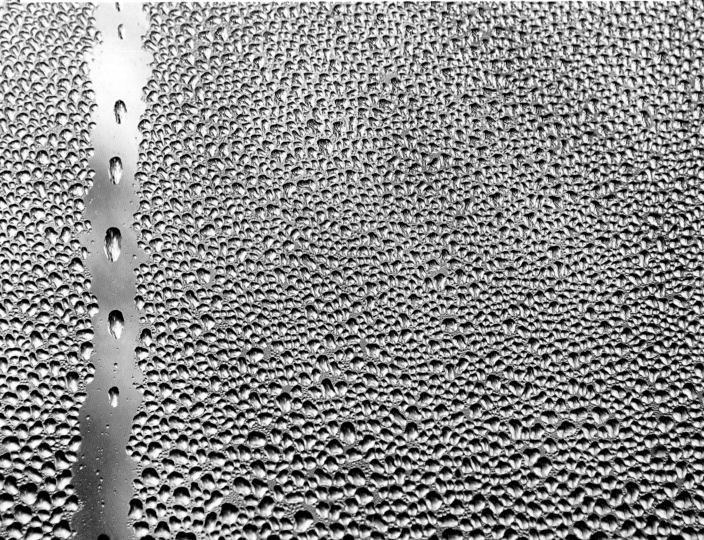

Unlike some other materials, water has no effect on glass. Water stays on the surface of glass.

Glass is waterproof.
Windows are made
from glass so rain
cannot get through!

13

Glass in Heat

Glass is made from sand. When sand is heated to a very high temperature, it turns into a liquid.

While it is liquid, the glass can be changed into different shapes.

This is called glass blowing.

Some toys are made from glass. Marbles are made from lots of layers of glass.

Can you think of any other toys that are made from glass?

Marbles have been used as toys for hundreds of years.

How many different games can you think of that use marbles?

Being Safe with Glass

Glass can be very dangerous. When glass is broken, the pieces can be very sharp to touch.

BE CAREFUL!
Do not touch.

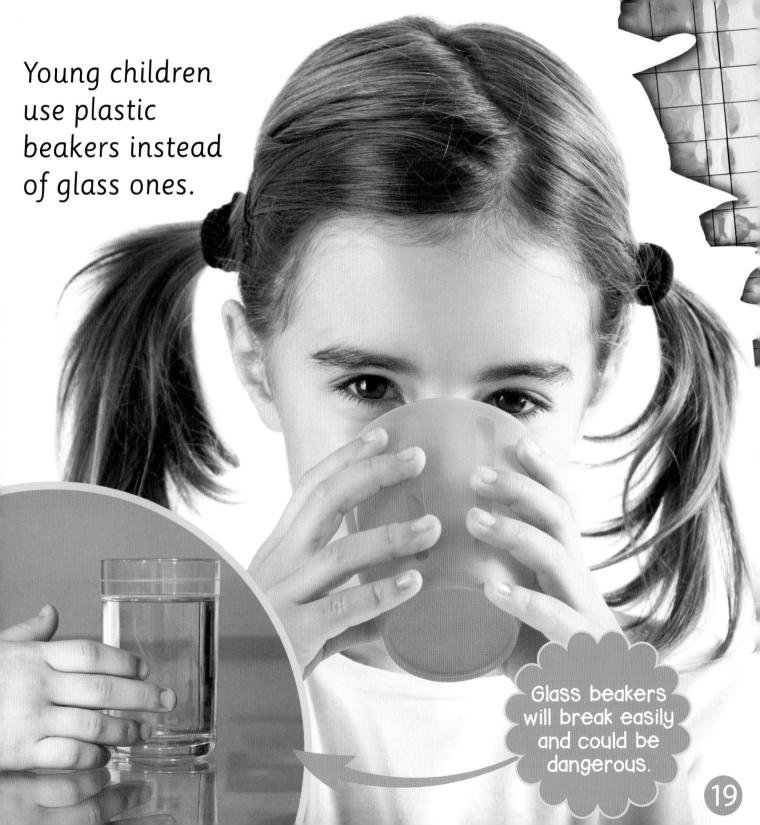

Young children use plastic beakers instead of glass ones.

Glass beakers will break easily and could be dangerous.

19

Recycling Glass

Glass can be recycled. This means we can use it again. Recycling helps us to care for our planet.

This symbol means that a material can be recycled!

To recycle glass, you should take your jars and bottles to special bottle banks.

Fun Facts

Make a list of all the things you can think of that are made from glass. Write their properties next to them.

Are they strong or fragile?

Are they shiny or dull?

Most families use around 330 glass bottles and jars every year!

Recycling one glass bottle saves enough energy to power a computer for 25 minutes!

Glossary

Fragile
Something that is easily broken.

Man-made
Something that is made by humans.

Natural
Something that has been made by nature.

Properties
The different qualities of a material.

Shatter
When something is broken into pieces.

Surface
The outside part of something.

Waterproof
Not affected by water. Water cannot get through.

Index

Photocredits: Abbreviations: l-left, r-right, b-bottom, t-top, c-centre, m-middle. All images are courtesy of Shutterstock.com.
Front Cover - Vladitto. Front Cover bl - Iaroslav Neliubov. Front Cover bm – Lollo. Front Cover br - Dabarti CGI. 2 – GlebStock. 3 – TigerForce. 4t – 3445128471. 4bl – Temych. 4bm - Sunny studio. 4br – Pressmaster. 5bl – wavebreakmedia. 5r – hartphotography. 6l - S_Photo. 6r – PlusONE. 7 – MNStudio. 8 – Halfpoint. 9l - Diana Taliun. 9r - Iaroslav Neliubov. 10 - Tom Gowanlock. 11l – alexkatkov. 11inset - Dabarti CGI. 12 - Denis Tabler. 13 – romakoma. 14 - Martin Valigursky. 15 – CREATISTA. 16 - CreativeNature R.Zwerver. 17 – auremar. 18 - r.classen. 18inset - KPG_Payless. 19 - Renata Sedmakova. 19inset – iko. 20 - Matic Stojs. 21 - Switlana Yaremenko. 22t - Somchai Som. 22bl - Tamas Panczel – Eross. 22bl - Africa Studio. 22br – Kmannn. 24 - Serhiy Kobyakov.